Light Through the Windows

The Stained-Glass Windows of
Salem Congregational Church
Scottsbluff, Nebraska

Dale Henry Brown

3

Dedication

"Light Through the Windows" is dedicated to all the precious souls who have been a part of Salem Congregational Church since its organization in 1928. Their labor of love as ministers and laypersons has, in itself, been a light shining in our community.

Light Through the Windows

In the beginning, God created the heavens and the earth. The earth was without form and void, and darkness was over the face of the deep. And the spirit of God was hovering over the face of the waters. And God said, "Let there be light," and there was light. And God saw that the light was good. And God separated the light from the darkness. God called the light Day, and the darkness he called Night. And there were evening and there was morning, the first day. (Genesis 1:1-4)

This book is about light. Light shining through skillfully crafted windows into pictures portraying the life of Christ and his kingdom. The light shines through from the sun to expose the beauty of the glass, but it also shines through to enlighten the beauty of the Son who is the Way, and the Truth, and the Life, our Lord Jesus Christ.

A Brief History of Stained-Glass Windows

Stained-glass windows have been around for centuries. A Benedictine priest born in Northumbria, England, is credited with the earliest known construction of stained-glass windows around 628 A.D. Benedict Biscop was the founder and first Abbott of the celebrated twin monasteries of Saints Peter and Paul at Wearmouth, Northumbria and nearby Jarrow on Tyne. He is considered to be the father of Benedictine monasticism in England. When building the monastery of St. Peter, he commissioned workmen from France to glaze the windows. This is perhaps the beginning of stained-glass windows in cathedrals and churches that have served to illustrate the narratives of the Bible and have inspired and moved people's hearts to worship the God we serve. The creation of the windows themselves is an act of worship.

The Windows of Salem

The stained-glass windows pictured in this book were not part of the original construction of Salem Congregational Church in Scottsbluff, Nebraska, which was constructed in 1962. The beautiful stained-glass windows gracing the east and west walls of the sanctuary were installed in 1977-78 by Hauser Studios of Stained Glass, Inc. located in Winona, Minnesota for a total cost of about $12,000.

A section of the contractual agreement with Hauser Studios details the materials used for the windows.

"Imported antique glasses from Germany, England or France, and the finest cathedral glasses will be used in the fabrication of these windows. Any painted work on the windows will be hand-painted and kiln-fired so as to become permanently fused into the glass itself.

Each piece of glass will be bound in pre-stretched lead cames [the lead channels the glass fits in] with each joint firmly soldered inside and out. All windows will be set in lead binders and securely braced where necessary with 1/8" thick flat steel reinforcing braces soldered to the lead joints for firmness and permanence. A special elastic glazing compound will be forcibly brushed into the grooves around each piece of glass, inside and out, assuring an elastic setting and a tight weather seal.

3/16" clear Lexan will be installed over each of the units, and is included in the price below."

Each one of the windows herein is featured individually along with an explanation of their meaning and a devotional application. It is my prayer that you will be blessed and inspired by the beauty of each window and that you will be drawn into a deeper walk with our Lord Jesus Christ as you meditate upon their meaning.

Window Locations

As you stand to face the front of the sanctuary, windows on the left are on the East side, windows on the right are on the West side. As we turn toward the East wall, our story begins with the top left window depicting the birth of Jesus. We then look at the lower window in the same frame. We will continue our journey following the same pattern (upper, then lower) moving to the right. When we complete viewing the East wall, we will turn around and begin with the top right window, moving left until we end with the lower window at the front of the sanctuary. With one minor correction (which will be pointed out at its occurrence) the windows follow a chronological journey of the life of Christ.

Window 1

The wonderful Christmas story is depicted in this window. The symbolism is beautiful and significant. We see a star with its rays shining down on the manger. In the center is what appears to be a large P which extends down into a large X. The P and X form what is known as Chi-Rho.

Notice that the star has five points, a symbol of the Star of Bethlehem and represents Jesus' birth and incarnation.

> *I see him, but not now;*
> *I behold him, but not near:*
> *a star shall come out of Jacob.*
> *(Numbers 24:17)*

The Chi-Rho (pronounced "KEE-roe") is a Christian symbol consisting of the intersection of the Greek capital letters Chi (X) and Rho

(P), which are the first two letters of "Christ" in Greek (ΧΡΙΣΤΟΣ, Christos). The Chi-Rho can represent either Christ or Christianity and is also known as a Christogram.

Read these words from Matthew, Chapter 1:18-25:

18 Now the birth of Jesus Christ took place in this way. When his mother Mary had been betrothed to Joseph, before they came together she was found to be with child from the Holy Spirit. 19 And her husband Joseph, being a just man and unwilling to put her to shame, resolved to divorce her quietly. 20 But as he considered these things, behold, an angel of the Lord appeared to him in a dream, saying, "Joseph, son of David, do not fear to take Mary as your wife, for that which is conceived in her is from the Holy Spirit. 21 She will bear a son, and you shall call his name Jesus, for he will save his people from their sins." 22 All this took place to fulfill what the Lord had spoken by the prophet:

23 "Behold, the virgin shall conceive and bear a son,
    and they shall call his name Immanuel"

(which means, God with us). [24] *When Joseph woke from sleep, he did as the angel of the Lord commanded him: he took his wife,* [25] *but knew her not until she had given birth to a son. And he called his name Jesus.*

As you contemplate the beauty of this marvelous window allow the light to shine from that star into your heart.

Father, thank you for the gift of Jesus. He is the light of the world and the light of my life. Help me let his light shine through me today. Amen.

Window 2

The familiar story of the wise men bringing their gifts to the Savior is depicted in Window 2. The gifts are depicted as three containers representing gold, frankincense, and myrrh.

[1] Now after Jesus was born in Bethlehem of Judea in the days of Herod the king, behold, wise men from the east came to Jerusalem, [2] saying, "Where is he who has been born king of the Jews? For we saw his star when it rose and have come to worship him." [3] When Herod the king heard this, he was troubled, and all Jerusalem with him; [4] and assembling all the chief priests and scribes of the people, he inquired of them where the Christ was to be born. [5] They told him, "In Bethlehem of Judea, for so it is written by the prophet:

6 "'And you, O Bethlehem, in the land of Judah,
*   are by no means least among the rulers of Judah;*
for from you shall come a ruler
*   who will shepherd my people Israel.'"*

7 Then Herod summoned the wise men secretly and ascertained from them what time the star had appeared. 8 And he sent them to Bethlehem, saying, "Go and search diligently for the child, and when you have found him, bring me word, that I too may come and worship him." 9 After listening to the king, they went on their way. And behold, the star that they had seen when it rose went before them until it came to rest over the place where the child was. 10 When they saw the star, they rejoiced exceedingly with great joy. 11 And going into the house, they saw the child with Mary his mother, and they fell down and worshiped him. Then, opening their treasures, they offered him gifts, gold and frankincense and myrrh. 12 And being warned in a dream not to return to Herod, they departed to their own country by another way. (Matthew 2:1-12)

We do not know the exact number of these so-called "wise men," but it is commonly accepted that there were three because of the three gifts that were presented. It is also worth noting that Joseph and his family were now living in a house in Bethlehem indicating that the arrival of the wise men occurred after the young family left the stable.

It has been suggested that the three gifts were significant for Jesus: gold representing his kingship, frankincense a symbol of his priestly role, and myrrh a prefiguring of his death and embalming—an interpretation made popular in the well-known Christmas carol "We Three Kings."

Frankincense (also known as Olibanum) is an aromatic resin used in incense and perfumes, obtained from trees of the genus Boswellia in the family Burseraceae. Frankincense is a symbol of holiness and righteousness. The gift of frankincense to the Christ child was symbolic of his willingness to become a sacrifice, wholly giving himself up, analogous to a burnt offering. (see also Exodus 30:34; Leviticus 2:1, 2:16, 6:15, 24:7). The essential oil is obtained by steam distillation of the dry resin.

Myrrh (from the Aramaic language), is a natural gum or resin extracted from a number of small, thorny tree species of the genus Commiphora. Myrrh resin has been used throughout history as a perfume, incense, and medicine. Myrrh mixed with wine can also be ingested.

When a tree's wound penetrates through the bark and into the sapwood, the tree bleeds a resin. Myrrh gum, like frankincense, is such a resin.

Lord, "Let my prayer be counted as incense before you, Let and the lifting up of my hands as the evening sacrifice!" Amen. *(Psalm 141:2)*

Window 3

Window 3 shows the Star of David hovering over a basket containing two birds. The symbolism here is beautiful and well-conceived. This window is depicting the dedication of Jesus in the temple 40 days after his birth.

> *22 And when the time came for their purification according to the law of Moses, they brought him up to Jerusalem to present him to the Lord 23 (as it is written in the law of the Lord, "Every male who first opens the womb shall be called holy to the Lord")24 and to offer a sacrifice according to what is said in the law of the Lord, "a pair of turtledoves, or two young pigeons." (Luke 2:22-24)*

From this passage, we learned that Joseph was not a wealthy man. In fact, he must have been quite poor. The original command in the law of Moses required the sacrifice of a lamb but allowed the substitution of two turtledoves or young pigeons if the family was poor.

> *"...and he shall offer it before the Lord and make atonement for her then she shall be clean from the flow of her blood. This is the law for her who bears a child, either male or female. And if she cannot afford a lamb, then she shall take two turtledoves or two pigeons, one for a burnt offering and the other for a sin offering. And the priest shall make atonement for her, and she shall be clean." (Leviticus 12:7-8)*

The Star of David indicates that Mary and Joseph were observing their Jewish religious obligations and is also emblematic of Jesus (the Messiah) being the descendent of David as prophesied.

> *When your days are fulfilled, and you [David] lie down with your fathers, I will raise up your offspring after you, who shall come from your body, and I will establish his kingdom. He shall build a house for my name, and I will establish*

*the throne of his kingdom forever. (2
Samuel 7:12-13)*

The basket under the Star of David containing
the two turtledoves represents the offering
Mary and Joseph brought to present to the
priest for the dedication ceremony.

There were two other people at the dedication
of Jesus who must be recognized for our story
to be complete.

*25 Now there was a man in Jerusalem,
whose name was Simeon, and this man
was righteous and devout, waiting for
the consolation of Israel, and the Holy
Spirit was upon him. And it had been
revealed to him by the Holy Spirit that
he would not see death before he had
seen the Lord's Christ. 26 And it had
been revealed to him by the Holy Spirit
that he would not see death before he
had seen the Lord's Christ. 27 And he
came in the Spirit into the temple, and
when the parents brought in the child
Jesus, to do for him according to the
custom of the Law, 28 he took him up in
his arms and blessed God and said,*

*29 "Lord, now you are letting your
servant depart in peace,
    according to your word;
30 for my eyes have seen your salvation*

31 that you have prepared in the presence of all peoples,
32 a light for revelation to the Gentiles, and for glory to your people Israel."

33 And his father and his mother marveled at what was said about him. 34 And Simeon blessed them and said to Mary his mother, "Behold, this child is appointed for the fall and rising of many in Israel, and for a sign that is opposed 35 (and a sword will pierce through your own soul also), so that thoughts from many hearts may be revealed." (Luke 2:25-35)

This had to have been an amazing event for Mary and Joseph; another confirmation and reminder of who their precious child was. Now let's meet the other individual who shared in the dedication of Jesus.

36 And there was a prophetess, Anna, the daughter of Phanuel, of the tribe of Asher. She was advanced in years, having lived with her husband seven years from when she was a virgin, 37 and then as a widow until she was eighty-four. She did not depart from the temple, worshiping with fasting and prayer night and day. 38 And coming up at that very hour she began to give thanks to God and to speak of him to all who were waiting for the redemption of Jerusalem.

[39] And when they had performed everything according to the Law of the Lord, they returned into Galilee, to their own town of Nazareth. 40 And the child grew and became strong, filled with wisdom. And the favor of God was upon him. (Luke 2:36-40)

Imagine Mary holding her baby close to her as they made their way back to their hometown of Nazareth, her mind reeling with thoughts of what happened in the temple. Let us also imagine and let our minds reel with what that baby ultimately did for us by dying on the cross for our sins and giving us hope.

Father in heaven, what a blessed hope we have in Jesus. Simeon and Anna rejoiced to see the long-awaited blessing you promised. That baby did, indeed, fulfill all their desires. He has fulfilled my desires too, and I want my life to show my gratitude as fervently as Simeon and Anna. Amen.

Window 4

Window 4 beautifully depicts the baptism of Jesus by John the Baptist. John the Baptist had been preaching a gospel of repentance calling people to turn from their wicked ways and do what was right. So, it was a bit of a surprise to him when Jesus, who he apparently recognized as the Messiah, came to him to be baptized. Let's read the narrative as found in the Gospel of Matthew.

> *13 Then Jesus came from Galilee to the Jordan to John, to be baptized by him. 14 John would have prevented him, saying, "I need to be baptized by you, and do you come to me?" 15 But Jesus answered him, "Let it be so now, for thus it is fitting for us to fulfill all righteousness." Then he consented. 16 And when Jesus was baptized, immediately he went up from the water,*

*and behold, the heavens were opened
to him, and he saw the Spirit of God
descending like a dove and coming to
rest on him; ¹⁷ and behold, a voice from
heaven said, "This is my beloved Son,
with whom I am well pleased."
(Matthew 3:13-17)*

According to the gospel of Luke (3:23), Jesus
was about 30 years old when he was baptized.
Why did Jesus need to be baptized, a question
John the Baptist essentially asked him? Jesus
replied, *"Let it be so now, for thus it is fitting
for us to fulfill all righteousness."* Jesus was
baptized to show his complete willingness to
do the will of his father, to complete the
mission he had come to do. Billy Graham
offers us a good comment about this.

*"No, Jesus didn't need to repent of his sins,
because in all the history of the human race
He alone was completely sinless. The reason is
because He was God in human flesh, sent
from heaven on that first Christmas to save us
from our sins.*

*Why, then, did Jesus seek out John and be
baptized by him in the Jordan river? (You can
read the Bible's account of this in Matthew
3:13-17.) The reason is because Jesus — who
was the sinless Son of God — took upon*

Himself your sins and my sins, and the sins of the whole human race. Just as He didn't have to die, so He didn't have to be baptized — until He became the bearer of all our sins. This He did by coming to earth for us.

In other words, from the very beginning of His ministry, Jesus demonstrated that He was the promised Messiah, and (in the words of John the Baptist) "the Lamb of God, who takes away the sin of the world!" (John 1:29). His baptism was a sign of this great truth — and it was confirmed immediately by a voice from heaven declaring, "This is my Son, whom I love; with him, I am well pleased" (Matthew 3:17).

No, Jesus didn't need to repent — but we do, for we have sinned, and our only hope is Christ and His sacrifice for us. Have you opened your heart and life to His forgiveness and His cleansing power?*

This brings us to the artistic portrayal in Window 4.

Here we see a dove descending upon a cross with a rather peculiar looking symbol fanning out from it toward the water below. The dove is easy to explain as a symbol of the Holy

Spirit. The cross is also understandable, but what is that symbol in the middle? It was somewhat baffling to me until I counted the number of beams coming out of it: seven. Seven is the number of completeness and perfection (both physical and spiritual). Remember what the voice from heaven said? *"This is my beloved son, with whom I am well pleased."*

Jesus was the complete, sinless man who was to become the "lamb without blemish" as a sacrifice for the sins of all people. As you gaze upon this window let the fullness of that truth impact your life.

Lord, it was pure love that sent Jesus to this world to suffer and die for my sins. His baptism shows that he was willing. Thank you, Jesus! May I be willing to give my all to you in love and obedience. Amen.

*billygraham.org

Window 5

One day Jesus was walking along the Sea of Galilee. He wasn't out for just a leisurely morning stroll enjoying the warmth of the sun and the lapping of the waves against the shoreline. He was on a mission. It was time for him to begin his ministry and he was looking for team members. He saw a couple of fellows in a boat a short way off the shore putting nets into the water looking for a morning catch. Jesus shouted to them, *"Come and follow me and I will make you fishers of men."* Amazingly, the Bible says these two men left their nets and followed Jesus. Peter and Andrew became his first disciples. (See Matthew 4:18-22)

Jesus calling his disciples is what is pictured in Window 5. Here, we see a cross with the top forming what looks like a P. As mentioned in our discussion of Window 1, the P is the Greek letter "Rho." The cross itself forms the letter T which in the Greek is "Tau." This combination was used because it symbolized the cross with a person on it. It is called a staurogram and was used by scribes as an abbreviation in manuscripts for the cross.

Now take a close look at the net. How many fish do you see? There are nine. In Bible numerology nine is seen as a multiple of three symbolizing divine completeness or the finality of faith. When did Christ die? In the ninth hour (3 pm). Yom Kippur occurs on the 9th day of the 7th month (Lev. 23:32).

But perhaps, more importantly, the nine fish could represent the fruit of the Spirit which would manifest itself in the disciples in days to come.

> But the fruit of the Spirit is love, joy, peace, patience, kindness, goodness, faithfulness, gentleness, self-control; against such things there is no law. (Galatians 5:22-23)

So, to sum up the images in this window, we are called to be disciples of Christ by coming to the cross and acknowledging that Jesus has died for our sins, repent of our sins, and follow him. In his "net" our lives will be changed, and we will begin to bear the fruit of the Holy Spirit becoming a blessing to our heavenly Father and those with whom we have contact in the world.

Lord, thank you for the call of Jesus in my life. Following him is the most important decision I have made. May my heart be fertile soil for the fruit of the Holy Spirit to grow and be a blessing to others. Amen.

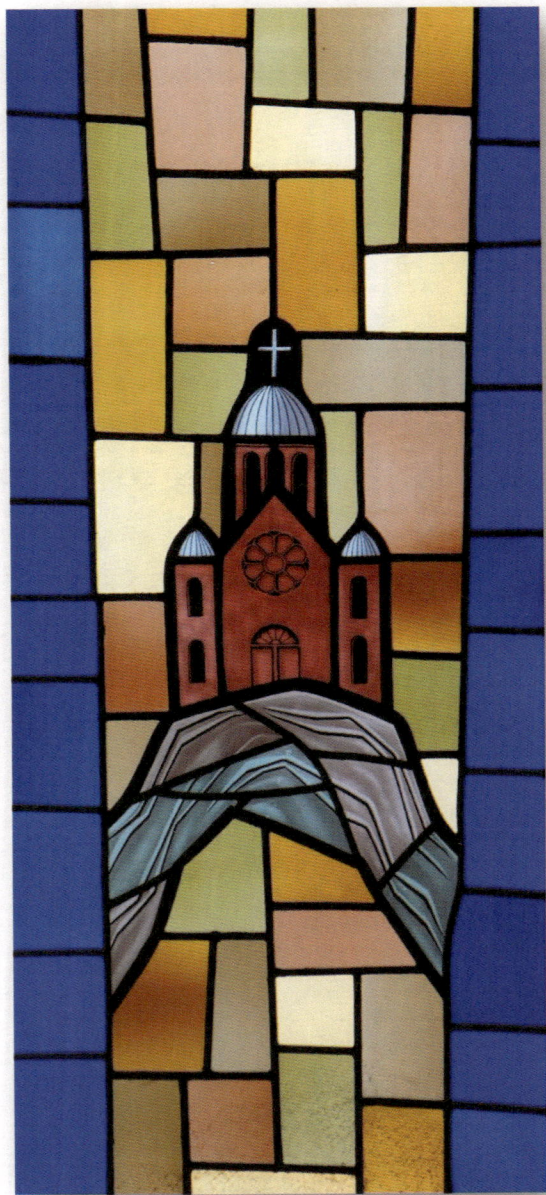

Window 6

The understanding of Window 6 is pretty straightforward. Here we see pictured a church built upon a rock. It is based upon the following Scripture.

> [13] Now when Jesus came into the district of Caesarea Philippi, he asked his disciples, "Who do people say that the Son of Man is?" [14] And they said, "Some say John the Baptist, others say Elijah, and others Jeremiah or one of the prophets." [15] He said to them, "But who do you say that I am?" [16] Simon Peter replied, "You are the Christ, the Son of the living God." [17] And Jesus answered him, "Blessed are you, Simon Bar-Jonah! For flesh and blood has not revealed this to you, but my Father who is in heaven. [18] And I tell you, you are Peter, and on this rock I will build my church, and the gates of hell shall not

prevail against it. ¹⁹ I will give you the keys of the kingdom of heaven, and whatever you bind on earth shall be bound in heaven, and whatever you loose on earth shall be loosed in heaven." ²⁰ Then he strictly charged the disciples to tell no one that he was the Christ. (Matthew 16:13-20)

This passage is known as Peter's Great Confession. Biblical scholars have varying viewpoints on what Jesus meant when he said, *"on this rock, I will build my church."* Some have taught that he was referring to Peter as the rock and hence he became the first pope. It is interesting to note that even though Peter's name means "rock (Petros)," when Jesus said, "on this rock," he used the Greek feminine word for rock (Petra). In other words, Jesus was saying the church, the Bride of Christ, would be built upon himself.

On the other hand, there is a sense in which Peter fits these words of Jesus. William Barclay writes:

It is that Peter himself Is the rock, but in a special sense. He is not the rock on which the Church is founded; that rock is God. He is the first stone of the whole Church. Peter was the first person on earth to discover who Jesus *was; he was the first person to make the leap of faith and see in him the Son of the living God. In other words, Peter was the first member of the Church, and, in that sense, the whole church is built on him. It is as if Jesus said to Peter: "Peter, you are the first person to grasp who I am; you are there for the first stone, the foundation stone, the very beginning of the church which I am founding." And in ages to come, everyone who makes the same discovery as Peter is another stone added into the edifice of the Church of Christ.* *

As I pondered this great confession of Peter, I remembered another confession he made that has encouraged me many times as I have struggled with my faith. It is recorded in the sixth chapter of John's Gospel. Jesus had been teaching, referring to himself as the bread of life. He stated:

> [53] *"Truly, truly, I say to you, unless you eat the flesh of the Son of Man and drink his blood, you have no life in you.* [54] *Whoever feeds on my flesh and drinks my blood has eternal life, and I will raise him up on the last day.* [55] *For my flesh is true food, and my blood is true drink.* [56] *Whoever feeds on my flesh and drinks my blood abides in me, and I in him.* [57] *As the living Father sent*

me, and I live because of the Father, so whoever feeds on me, he also will live because of me. [58] This is the bread that came down from heaven, not like the bread the fathers ate, and died. Whoever feeds on this bread will live forever." (John 6:53-58)

We understand his words now in the context of Holy Communion in which we partake of the bread and drink the wine representing his body and blood he gave for us by dying on the cross. (We will look at this in more detail when we look at Window 10). But when he spoke those words in the Jewish synagogue, it caused many to take offense.

*[66] After this many of his disciples turned back and no longer walked with him. [67] So Jesus said to the twelve, "Do you want to go away as well?" [68] Simon Peter answered him, **"Lord, to whom shall we go? You have the words of eternal life, and we have believed, [69] and have come to know, that you are the Holy One of God."** (Emphasis added) (John 6:66-69)*

Indeed, there is nowhere else we can go to find eternal life!

The most important take away I see for this window is how we answer the question Jesus put to his disciples, "But who do you say that I am?" My prayer is that you will be able to say with Peter, *"You are the Christ, the Son of the living God."* When you do, you become a rock in the building of the church of our Lord Jesus Christ.

Father, there is something deep down inside me that stirs when I proclaim the words of Peter, "You are the Christ, the Son of the living God." What joy, what peace, what assurance wells up within! Bless your name! Amen.

*William BARCLAY. The Gospel of Matthew, Volume 2: The New Daily Study Bible (Kindle Location 2684). Westminster John Knox Press. Kindle Edition.

Window 7

As we gaze upon Window 7, we immediately see a representation of the 10 Commandments. In Deuteronomy 19 we find a clue to what is taking place in this scene that is commonly referred to as the Transfiguration of Jesus.

> "A single witness shall not suffice against a person for any crime or for any wrong in connection with any offense that he has committed. Only on the evidence of two witnesses or of three witnesses shall a charge be established." (Deuteronomy 19:15)

Keep that thought in mind as we read the account of the Transfiguration of Jesus as found in Mark's gospel.

> 2 And after six days Jesus took with him Peter and James and John, and led

*them up a high mountain by
themselves. And he was transfigured
before them, [3] and his clothes became
radiant, intensely white, as no one on
earth could bleach them. [4] And there
appeared to them Elijah with Moses,
and they were talking with Jesus. [5] And
Peter said to Jesus, "Rabbi, it is good
that we are here. Let us make three
tents, one for you and one for Moses
and one for Elijah." [6] For he did not
know what to say, for they were
terrified. [7] And a cloud overshadowed
them, and a voice came out of the
cloud, "This is my beloved Son; listen to
him." [8] And suddenly, looking around,
they no longer saw anyone with them
but Jesus only.*

*[9] And as they were coming down the
mountain, he charged them to tell no
one what they had seen, until the Son
of Man had risen from the dead. [10] So
they kept the matter to themselves,
questioning what this rising from the
dead might mean.*

In Window 7 we have the Chi-Rho (the Greek
abbreviation for Christ) embedded in light,
representing Christ in his glorified state. To
the left is a depiction of the 10
Commandments, representing Moses, and a

chariot of fire on the right representing Elijah the prophet.

According to the law of "two or three witnesses," we actually have two sets of three in this story giving testimony to the transfiguration and glory of our Lord Jesus Christ. First, there are Moses, Elijah, and the voice of God. Second, there are Peter, James, and John.

"The word "transfigured" is a very interesting word. The Greek word is "metamorpho" and it means to transform, literally or figuratively to metamorphose, or to change. The word is a verb that means to change into another form. It also means to change the outside to match the inside. The prefix "meta" means to change, and the "morphe" means form. In the case of the transfiguration of Jesus Christ, it means to match the outside with the reality of the inside. To change the outward so that it matches the inward reality. Jesus' divine nature was "veiled" (Hebrews 10:20) in human form, and the transfiguration was a glimpse of that glory. Therefore, the transfiguration of Jesus Christ displayed the Shekinah glory of God incarnate in the Son. The voice of God attesting to the truth of

Jesus' Sonship was the second time God's voice was heard. The first time was at Jesus' baptism into His public ministry by John the Baptist (Matthew 3:7; Mark 1:11; Luke 3:22)."*

What a glorious experience for Peter, James, and John! We can only imagine the excitement they must have felt as they witnessed Jesus being glorified before their eyes and these two patriarchs coming alongside to visit. But the lesson they carried with them back down the mountain was found in the voice that came out of the clouds, *"This is my beloved son; listen to him."* This should be our focus. Jesus is the center of our life and the one to whom we should always look.

> *1 Therefore, since we are surrounded by so great a cloud of witnesses, let us also lay aside every weight, and sin which clings so closely, and let us run with endurance the race that is set before us, 2 looking to Jesus, the founder and perfecter of our faith, who for the joy that was set before him endured the cross, despising the shame, and is seated at the right hand of the throne of God. 3 Consider him who endured from sinners such hostility against himself, so*

that you may not grow weary or fainthearted. (Hebrews 12:1-3)

Lord of my life, there are so many voices clamoring for my time, but if I keep Jesus at the center of all things, I know I will succeed in my walk with you. Never am I out of your care. Lead the way, gentle Savior. Amen

*www.allaboutjesuschrist.org, Transfiguration of Jesus Christ

Window 8

Palm branches are the unique feature in Window 8, which symbolizes the triumphal entry of Jesus into Jerusalem the week prior to his crucifixion.

A considerable amount of time was spent researching the symbolism in this window. I could find nothing, beyond the palm branches and cross, to explain the circle in the middle. There was simply no symbolism I could find of a ball shape with a bar running through it as depicted. I was about to chalk it up to the artist just creatively tying it together when I saw it. How precious! How wonderful! How creative! What did I see? Look at the window as a whole, not the individual parts. Can you see Jesus riding on the back of a donkey? The palm branches forming the donkey's ears?

After you see it, you will probably not see anything else!

Palm branches from ancient history were symbolic of victory. King Solomon used them in the decor of the temple.

> *Around all the walls of the house he carved engraved figures of cherubim and palm trees and open flowers, in the inner and outer rooms. (1 Kings 6:29)*

Perhaps the origination of palm branches being used on Palm Sunday goes back to the Jewish festival of Sukkoth when worshipers would waive palm branches and recite words from Psalm 118 as they processed through Jerusalem to the temple.[*]

Let's read the following account of the triumphal entry of Jesus into Jerusalem as found in Matthew 21:1-11.

[1] Now when they drew near to Jerusalem and came to Bethphage, to the Mount of Olives, then Jesus sent two disciples, [2] saying to them, "Go into the village in front of you, and immediately you will find a donkey tied, and a colt with her. Untie them and bring them to me. [3] If anyone says anything to you, you shall say, 'The Lord needs them,' and he will send them at once." [4] This took place to fulfill what was spoken by the prophet, saying,

[5] "Say to the daughter of Zion,
'Behold, your king is coming to you,
humble, and mounted on a donkey,
on a colt, the foal of a beast of burden.'"

[6] The disciples went and did as Jesus had directed them. [7] They brought the donkey and the colt and put on them their cloaks, and he sat on them. [8] Most of the crowd spread their cloaks on the road, and others cut branches from the trees and spread them on the road. [9] And the crowds that went before him and that followed him were shouting, "Hosanna to the Son of David! Blessed

is he who comes in the name of the Lord! Hosanna in the highest!" [10] And when he entered Jerusalem, the whole city was stirred up, saying, "Who is this?" [11] And the crowds said, "This is the prophet Jesus, from Nazareth of Galilee."

You will also find this account in Mark 11:1-11, Luke 19:28-44, and John 12:12-15.

The victory celebration in heaven in the book of Revelation also includes palm branches.

[9] After this I looked, and behold, a great multitude that no one could number, from every nation, from all tribes and peoples and languages, standing before the throne and before the Lamb, clothed in white robes, with palm branches in their hands, [10] and crying out with a loud voice, "Salvation belongs to our God who sits on the throne, and to the Lamb!" (Revelation 7:9-10)

When we look at this window, let us contemplate the glorious victory we have through our Lord Jesus Christ. Let us join with the apostle Paul who said:

But one thing I do: forgetting what lies behind and straining forward to what lies ahead, I press on toward the goal for the prize of the upward call of God in Christ Jesus. (Philippians 3:13b-14)

Father, I thank you for the victory I have in Jesus. Yes, I am fighting a battle for survival in this world, and there are many challenges. But the truth is, even though there are battles to be fought, the outcome is already determined, having been won on the cross. Glorious victory! Amen.

*Dick Harfield: christianity.stackexchange.com, What Is The Significance of Palm Branches

Window 9

Just before Jesus went to the cross, he spent time with his disciples in the Garden of Gethsemane. This is what Window 9 symbolizes. In the order of windows, it is actually one step out of place. Window 10 represents the Lord's Supper, which occurred prior to the Gethsemane experience. Be that as it may, we will discuss the windows in the order they are framed.

We will find the account of Gethsemane mentioned in all four gospels. Let's read the narrative from the Gospel of Mark 14:32-42.

> *32 And they went to a place called Gethsemane. And he said to his disciples, "Sit here while I pray." 33 And he took with him Peter and James and John, and began to be greatly distressed and troubled. 34 And he said*

to them, "My soul is very sorrowful, even to death. Remain here and watch." 35 And going a little farther, he fell on the ground and prayed that, if it were possible, the hour might pass from him. 36 And he said, "Abba, Father, all things are possible for you. Remove this cup from me. Yet not what I will, but what you will." 37 And he came and found them sleeping, and he said to Peter, "Simon, are you asleep? Could you not watch one hour? 38 Watch and pray that you may not enter into temptation. The spirit indeed is willing, but the flesh is weak." 39 And again he went away and prayed, saying the same words. 40 And again he came and found them sleeping, for their eyes were very heavy, and they did not know what to answer him. 41 And he came the third time and said to them, "Are you still sleeping and taking your rest? It is enough; the hour has come. The Son of Man is betrayed into the hands of sinners. 42 Rise, let us be going; see, my betrayer is at hand."

Looking at the window, we see the "Chi" (X) representing Christ. In its center is a cross, both are resting on a challis (cup). Here in the Garden of Gethsemane Jesus fought his ultimate battle with his humanity. In verse 38 he tells his disciples, *"the spirit indeed is willing, but the flesh is weak."* He was referring to their falling asleep instead of keeping watch as he had commanded. But on a greater level, he fully understood how weak the flesh was. Everything in him that was human rebelled against what lay ahead while everything in him that was divine rebelled against turning back. The struggle showed that he was fully human. Humans have a natural aversion to pain. We do everything we can to avoid it. In this, Jesus struggled.

The Gospel of Luke provides an interesting point absent from the other gospels. The thrice repeated prayer of Jesus was, *"Father, if You are willing, remove this cup from Me; yet not My will, but Yours be done."* (Luke 22:42) Luke records that *"an angel from heaven appeared to Him, strengthening Him."* (vs. 43) This is reminiscent of the angels ministering to Jesus after his temptation in the wilderness at the beginning of his ministry (see Matthew 4:1-11).

I wonder how many times an angel comes along side us when we are facing the struggles of life. Perhaps as you are reading this, you are hurting, feeling alone and absent of hope.

Can you allow yourself to believe that even now, angels are standing near, protecting you as the Holy Spirit ministers to your need? Oh, dear child of God, as you gaze upon this window, look to him who suffered the agony of Gethsemane and the Cross.

> 21 "...Christ also suffered for you, leaving you an example, so that you might follow in his steps. 22 He committed no sin, neither was deceit found in his mouth. 23 When he was reviled, he did not revile in return; when he suffered, he did not threaten, but continued entrusting himself to him who judges justly. 24 He himself bore our sins in his body on the tree, that we might die to sin and live to righteousness. By his wounds you have been healed. 25 For you were straying like sheep, but have now returned to the Shepherd and Overseer of your souls." (1 Peter 2:21-25)

J. Vernon McGee comments on this "cup" of suffering Jesus was anguishing over.

"The cup, I think, was the cross, and I do not mean the suffering of death. The cup was that He was made sin for us. He is the Holy One of God. When my sin was put upon Him, it was repulsive. I do not know why we think we are

so attractive to God. My sin put upon Christ was repulsive and awful. It was terrible, and for a moment He rebelled against it. It was in the Garden of Gethsemane under the shadow of the cross that the Tempter came to offer the Lord once again the crown without the cross. The Lord, however, had come to do His Father's will and so He could say "nevertheless not my will, but thine, be done." He committed Himself to His Father's will, although bearing your sin and mine was so repulsive to Him."*

Dare to lift your voice even now and begin to praise him. Thank him for suffering for your sins! Thank him for the angels watching over you! Thank him for his Holy Spirit at work in your life just now! Don't quit until you sense the glory of his presence all around you.

Lord, and provider for my soul, I love you and thank you for the suffering Jesus endured on my behalf. Thank you for angels who watch over me, and your Holy Spirit abiding within to give me power for living. Amen.

*McGee, J. Vernon. Thru the Bible Commentary, Volumes 1-5: Genesis through Revelation (Thru the Bible 5 Volume Set) (Kindle Locations 99440-99444). Thomas Nelson. Kindle Edition.

Window 10

One of my favorite activities in the church is serving what we refer to as Communion. Churches observe this sacrament in various ways and times. In our congregation, we observe Communion (The Lord's Supper) typically the first Sunday of each month. Other churches may observe it every Sunday, still others only three or four times a year. But whenever it is observed in evangelical churches, it serves the same purpose of bringing us together in remembrance of Jesus.

The occasion on which Jesus implemented this sacrament is depicted in Window 10. Here we see a chalice with the Chi-Rho resting above it in the center of a circle with six crosses on each side. In the life of Christ, what does the number 12 bring to mind? You guessed it, the

12 disciples. Note that one of the crosses is a different color from the rest, certainly representing Judas, the one who betrayed Jesus for 30 pieces of silver. Let's read the account as recorded in Luke's gospel.

[3] Then Satan entered into Judas called Iscariot, who was of the number of the twelve. [4] He went away and conferred with the chief priests and officers how he might betray him to them. [5] And they were glad, and agreed to give him money. [6] So he consented and sought an opportunity to betray him to them in the absence of a crowd.

[7] Then came the day of Unleavened Bread, on which the Passover lamb had to be sacrificed. [8] So Jesus sent Peter and John, saying, "Go and prepare the Passover for us, that we may eat it." [9] They said to him, "Where will you have us prepare it?" [10] He said to them, "Behold, when you have entered the city, a man carrying a jar of water will meet you. Follow him into the house that he enters [11] and tell the master of the house, 'The Teacher says to you, Where is the guest room, where I may eat the Passover with my disciples?' [12] And he will show you a large upper room furnished; prepare it there." [13] And they went and found it just as he

had told them, and they prepared the Passover.

14 And when the hour came, he reclined at table, and the apostles with him. 15 And he said to them, "I have earnestly desired to eat this Passover with you before I suffer. 16 For I tell you I will not eat it until it is fulfilled in the kingdom of God." 17 And he took a cup, and when he had given thanks he said, "Take this, and divide it among yourselves. 18 For I tell you that from now on I will not drink of the fruit of the vine until the kingdom of God comes." 19 And he took bread, and when he had given thanks, he broke it and gave it to them, saying, "This is my body, which is given for you. Do this in remembrance of me." 20 And likewise the cup after they had eaten, saying, "This cup that is poured out for you is the new covenant in my blood. 21 But behold, the hand of him who betrays me is with me on the table. 22 For the Son of Man goes as it has been determined, but woe to that man by whom he is betrayed!" 23 And they began to question one another, which of them it could be who was going to do this. (Luke 22:3-23)

Matthew gives the details in answer to which of them it could be.

20 When it was evening, he reclined at table with the twelve. 21 And as they were eating, he said, "Truly, I say to you, one of you will betray me." 22 And they were very sorrowful and began to say to him one after another, "Is it I, Lord?" 23 He answered, "He who has dipped his hand in the dish with me will betray me. 24 The Son of Man goes as it is written of him, but woe to that man by whom the Son of Man is betrayed! It would have been better for that man if he had not been born." 25 Judas, who would betray him, answered, "Is it I, Rabbi?" He said to him, "You have said so." (Matthew 26:20-25)

The evening Jesus spent with his disciples around the table was not just another meal together with good friends. They were commemorating the Passover, the Jewish observance going all the way back to the Exodus when the Lord delivered the Israelites out of Egyptian bondage with the final plague when the Death Angel passed over the land killing the firstborn of man and beast. Only those who were in their houses with the blood of a lamb sprinkled over the doorpost were spared. (See Exodus 12)

This is our Passover celebration. Jesus became the sacrificial lamb whose blood was shed for our sins. We deserve death, but when we accept Jesus Christ as our personal savior, believing that he suffered and died for our sins, the Death Angel (so to speak) sees the blood on the cross and passes by.

Jerry Winfield writes:

Recently my wife and I had the opportunity to visit the battleship USS Missouri, which is now anchored off Ford Island in Pearl Harbor. Our tour of "Big Mo" ended at the place on the deck where General Douglas MacArthur accepted the unconditional surrender of the empire of Japan on September 2, 1945. This historic event ended the hostilities of World War II in the Pacific theater.

The signing of that treaty happened before my wife or I were born, but the events symbolized by that treaty shaped the world into which we were born and in which we now live. An event that happened more than 50 years ago still has significance. We still enjoy the freedoms secured by the heroic service of our parents and grandparents.

The God who acted in history to deliver His people Israel has also acted in history to deliver us. The elements used in the Supper *are not the real body and blood of Jesus but are powerful symbols that cause us to remember that Jesus really did suffer and die in a real, historical time and place. What Jesus did centuries ago impacts my life today and my eternity as well.**

Every time we come to the altar and partake of the bread and the cup we are reminded of Christ's sacrifice for our eternal life. Hallelujah! How can we not become overwhelmed with gratitude and joy as we observe this sacrament Jesus himself gave us? This window, Window 10, draws us to his great love.

Loving Father, the sacrament Jesus left us is a powerful reminder of what he did for us on the cross. It continually draws us to remember how precious our salvation is. Thank you. I love you, Jesus! Amen.

*Jerry Winfield: lifeway.com, A Call to Remember the Lord's Supper

Window 11

As we come to Windows 11 & 12, we reach the climax of our journey. All other windows flow into and out of these two. Window 11 illustrates the crucifixion of Jesus. Prayerfully read the account of the crucifixion from John 19.

> [16] So they took Jesus, [17] and he went out, bearing his own cross, to the place called The Place of a Skull, which in Aramaic is called Golgotha. [18] There they crucified him, and with him two others, one on either side, and Jesus between them. [19] Pilate also wrote an inscription and put it on the cross. It read, "Jesus of Nazareth, the King of the Jews." [20] Many of the Jews read this inscription, for the place where Jesus was crucified was near the city, and it

was written in Aramaic, in Latin, and in Greek. [21] So the chief priests of the Jews said to Pilate, "Do not write, 'The King of the Jews,' but rather, 'This man said, I am King of the Jews.'" [22] Pilate answered, "What I have written I have written."

[23] When the soldiers had crucified Jesus, they took his garments and divided them into four parts, one part for each soldier; also his tunic. But the tunic was seamless, woven in one piece from top to bottom, [24] so they said to one another, "Let us not tear it, but cast lots for it to see whose it shall be." This was to fulfill the Scripture which says,

"They divided my garments among them,
    and for my clothing they cast lots."

So the soldiers did these things, [25] but standing by the cross of Jesus were his mother and his mother's sister, Mary the wife of Clopas, and Mary Magdalene. [26] When Jesus saw his mother and the disciple whom he loved standing nearby, he said to his mother, "Woman, behold, your son!" [27] Then he said to the disciple, "Behold, your mother!" And from that hour the disciple took her to his own home.

28 After this, Jesus, knowing that all was now finished, said (to fulfill the Scripture), "I thirst." 29 A jar full of sour wine stood there, so they put a sponge full of the sour wine on a hyssop branch and held it to his mouth. 30 When Jesus had received the sour wine, he said, "It is finished," and he bowed his head and gave up his spirit.

31 Since it was the day of Preparation, and so that the bodies would not remain on the cross on the Sabbath (for that Sabbath was a high day), the Jews asked Pilate that their legs might be broken and that they might be taken away. 32 So the soldiers came and broke the legs of the first, and of the other who had been crucified with him. 33 But when they came to Jesus and saw that he was already dead, they did not break his legs. 34 But one of the soldiers pierced his side with a spear, and at once there came out blood and water. 35 He who saw it has borne witness—his testimony is true, and he knows that he is telling the truth—that you also may believe. 36 For these things took place that the Scripture might be fulfilled: "Not one of his bones will be broken." 37 And again another Scripture says, "They will look on him whom they have pierced." (John 19:16-37)

Let's look at each component represented. Remember the staurogram we learned about in Window 5? It appears again here in Window 11; the cross with the Greek letter Rho forming the top, representing a person on the cross. In this case, however, the letters INRI are accompanying it. INRI stems from the Latin phrase 'Iesus Nazarenus Rex Iudaeorum' meaning "Jesus of Nazareth, King of the Jews." This is the inscription Pilate had placed above Jesus' head. The Jewish leaders wanted him to change it to, "He said he was King of the Jews," but Pilate refused saying, "What I have written, I have written."

We also see in this window a lightning bolt. Lightning is not mentioned in any of the Gospels accounts of the crucifixion. What is mentioned is darkness and an earthquake. Perhaps the artist reasoned darkness in the middle of the day must have meant a severe storm accompanied with lightning. Let us accept that the lightning bolt represents the dramatic moment of Jesus' death when darkness fell, and an earthquake shook the ground.

In addition, we are told in Luke's gospel (23:44-45) at the moment of Jesus' death the large curtain in the temple that separated the Holy Place from the Holy of Holies was torn in two from top to bottom. Imagine the shock of whoever might have been standing nearby when it began to rip from the top!

"Christ's life was symbolized by the veil which actually shut out man from God in the Old Testament economy. When Christ died on the cross, the veil was torn in two so that the way to the Father was open!"*

> 19 *Therefore, brothers, since we have confidence to enter the holy places by the blood of Jesus,* 20 *by the new and living way that he opened for us through the curtain, that is, through his flesh,* 21 *and since we have a great priest over the house of God,* 22 *let us draw near with a true heart in full assurance of faith, with our hearts sprinkled clean from an evil conscience and our bodies washed with pure water.* 23 *Let us hold fast the confession of our hope without wavering, for he who promised is faithful.* 24 *And let us consider how to stir up one another to love and good works,* 25 *not neglecting to meet together, as is the habit of some, but encouraging one another, and all the more as you see the Day drawing near. (Hebrews 10:19-25)*

There are three crosses in Window 11. Two others were crucified with Jesus, one on the right and one on the left. All four gospels mention this. Matthew and Mark refer to them as robbers. Luke calls them criminals. John simply states, *"two other men."* Mark points out that this was a fulfillment of prophecy from Isaiah 53:12 which states the Messiah was *"numbered with the transgressors."*

It is interesting to note that even though Matthew and Mark indicate the two robbers mocked Jesus, Luke points out that one of them repented.

> *39 One of the criminals who was hanged railed at him, saying, "Are you not the Christ? Save yourself and us!" 40 But the other rebuked him, saying, "Do you not fear God since you are under the same sentence of condemnation? 41 And we indeed justly, for we are receiving the due reward of our deeds; but this man has done nothing wrong." 42 And he said, "Jesus, remember me when you come into your kingdom." 43 And he said to him, "Truly, I say to you, today you will be with me in paradise." (Luke 23:39-43)*

I can only imagine the joy that filled that man's soul when he was united with Jesus after death. Jesus told his disciples that there is joy in heaven when one person repents (Luke 15:7).

Beloved, have you thought of the joy in heaven over your salvation? If you have come to the cross and repented of your sins, acknowledging that Jesus suffered and died for your sins, you have been born again. Perhaps when you did that you experienced some kind of feeling, a feeling of relief, a burden lifted, joy in your spirit. Or perhaps your experience was not accompanied by any particular feeling. But I can tell you this, whether you experienced a feeling or not, there was joy in heaven! I am sure that if you would pause to think about that, you will have a sense of joy arise in your spirit. Spend some time just looking at and meditating upon this window with the following scripture in front of you.

"For God so loved the world, that he gave his only Son, that whoever believes in him should not perish but have eternal life. For God did not send his Son into the world to condemn the world, but in order that the world might be saved through him." (John 3:16-17)

Think about the fact that this window represents what Jesus did for you. Why did he do it? Because he loves you. Think of what he endured on your behalf; the mocking, ridicule, and pure pain and agony so that you can have eternal life. If it will help, pray this prayer:

Father in heaven, I acknowledge that I am a sinner and that Jesus died for my sins. I repent of my sins and accept the gift of life that Jesus paid for on the cross. Thank you for receiving me into your family as one of your children. Lead me and guide me in my walk with you as I grow to be more like Jesus. In His name, I pray. Amen.

*McGee, J. Vernon. Thru the Bible Commentary, Volumes 1-5: Genesis through Revelation (Thru the Bible 5 Volume Set) (Kindle Locations 99652-99654). Thomas Nelson. Kindle Edition.

Window 12

We now come to the second pivotal window, Window 12, depicting the resurrection of our Lord and Savior Jesus Christ. In this author's humble opinion, it is the most striking of all the windows. And indeed, it should be because the resurrection of Jesus means resurrection for all who believe in his matchless name. Before we look in detail at this window, let's read the Scripture that inspired it. Each of the Gospels records the resurrection, but we will read the account recorded in John 20:1-20.

> *[1] Now on the first day of the week Mary Magdalene came to the tomb early, while it was still dark, and saw that the stone had been taken away from the tomb. [2] So she ran and went to Simon Peter and the other disciple, the one*

whom Jesus loved, and said to them, "They have taken the Lord out of the tomb, and we do not know where they have laid him." ³ So Peter went out with the other disciple, and they were going toward the tomb. ⁴ Both of them were running together, but the other disciple outran Peter and reached the tomb first. ⁵ And stooping to look in, he saw the linen cloths lying there, but he did not go in. ⁶ Then Simon Peter came, following him, and went into the tomb. He saw the linen cloths lying there, ⁷ and the face cloth, which had been on Jesus' head, not lying with the linen cloths but folded up in a place by itself. ⁸ Then the other disciple, who had reached the tomb first, also went in, and he saw and believed; ⁹ for as yet they did not understand the Scripture, that he must rise from the dead. ¹⁰ Then the disciples went back to their homes.

¹¹ But Mary stood weeping outside the tomb, and as she wept, she stooped to look into the tomb. ¹² And she saw two angels in white, sitting where the body of Jesus had lain, one at the head and one at the feet. ¹³ They said to her, "Woman, why are you weeping?" She said to them, "They have taken away my Lord, and I do not know where they have laid him." ¹⁴ Having said this, she

turned around and saw Jesus standing, but she did not know that it was Jesus. ¹⁵ Jesus said to her, "Woman, why are you weeping? Whom are you seeking?" Supposing him to be the gardener, she said to him, "Sir, if you have carried him away, tell me where you have laid him, and I will take him away." ¹⁶ Jesus said to her, "Mary." She turned and said to him in Aramaic, "Rabboni!" (which means Teacher). ¹⁷ Jesus said to her, "Do not cling to me, for I have not yet ascended to the Father; but go to my brothers and say to them, 'I am ascending to my Father and your Father, to my God and your God.'" ¹⁸ Mary Magdalene went and announced to the disciples, "I have seen the Lord"— and that he had said these things to her.

¹⁹ On the evening of that day, the first day of the week, the doors being locked where the disciples were for fear of the Jews, Jesus came and stood among them and said to them, "Peace be with you." ²⁰ When he had said this, he showed them his hands and his side. Then the disciples were glad when they saw the Lord.

Resurrection day! What a day it was for his little band of followers. Two days earlier their lives of been turned upside down as they witnessed their beloved friend, their Lord, and Master cruelly abused and nailed to a Roman cross. Imagine what the scene was like as they were huddled together trying to figure out what they were going to do. How could they go on living without Jesus? Their sorrow and disappointment must have been overwhelming.

In the Gospel of Mark, we read that early in the morning of the third day, Mary Magdalene, Mary the mother of James, and Salome made their way to the tomb intending to anoint the body of Jesus with spices according to their custom. (Mark 16:1) As they went along, they discussed how they were going to get into the tomb. Who was going to roll the stone away for them? No need! The stone had already been rolled away. From then on, the day became more exciting culminating in Jesus appearing among them and saying, "Peace be with you."

Window 12 gloriously proclaims the resurrection of Jesus Christ. The tomb, with the stone laying aside, the cross extending away from it with the Christian flag proclaiming victory, a sunrise as a backdrop.

Since the artist chose to embed what we recognize as the "Christian Flag" in this window, perhaps it is appropriate to have a little history lesson on the origin of the Christian Flag.

"The Christian flag dates back to an impromptu speech given by Charles C. Overton, a Sunday school superintendent in New York, on September 26, 1897. The guest speaker for the Sunday school kick-off didn't show up, so Overton had to wing it. Spying an American flag near the podium, he started talking about flags and their symbolism. Along the way, he proposed that Christians should have their own flag—an idea that stayed on his mind long after the speech. In 1907 Overton teamed up with Ralph Diffendorfer, secretary to the Methodist Young People's Missionary Movement, to produce and promote the flag.

*The colors on the flag, not surprisingly, match those on the American flag. White represents purity and peace, blue indicates fidelity, and red stands for Christ's blood sacrifice."**

The flag in Window 12 proclaims the victory we have in Jesus Christ who conquered sin and the grave and gives us the freedom to live complete, God-filled lives.

12 Now if Christ is proclaimed as raised from the dead, how can some of you say that there is no resurrection of the dead? 13 But if there is no resurrection of the dead, then not even Christ has been raised. 14 And if Christ has not been raised, then our preaching is in vain, and your faith is in vain. 15 We are even found to be misrepresenting God, because we testified about God that he raised Christ, whom he did not raise if it is true that the dead are not raised. 16 For if the dead are not raised, not even Christ has been raised. 17 And if Christ has not been raised, your faith is futile, and you are still in your sins. 18 Then those also who have fallen asleep in Christ have perished. 19 If in Christ we have hope in this life only, we are of all people most to be pitied.

20 But in fact, Christ has been raised from the dead, the firstfruits of those who have fallen asleep. 21 For as by a man came death, by a man has come also the resurrection of the dead. 22 For as in Adam all die, so also in Christ shall all be made alive. 23 But each in his own order: Christ the firstfruits, then at his coming those who belong to Christ. 24

Then comes the end, when he delivers
the kingdom to God the Father after
destroying every rule and every
authority and power. (1 Corinthians
15:12-24)

Notice, also, that the flag is in the shape of an eagle's head. It is another sign of the victory we have in Jesus. There is an entire teaching about the "Eagle Christian." It brings to mind Isaiah 40:31:

...but those who hope in the Lord
    will renew their strength.
They will soar on wings like eagles;
    they will run and not grow weary,
    they will walk and not be faint.

When discouragement raises its ugly head, and you falter in your faith wondering where God is and why he isn't answering your prayers, just remember Christ is alive. He is the King of Kings and Lord of lords, and he has won the battle.

Even the great preacher Charles Spurgeon struggled with his faith, yet the resurrection power of Jesus Christ always saw him through.

"I am the subject of depression so fearful that I hope none of you ever get to such extremes of wretchedness as I go to. But I always get back again by this-I know that I trust Christ. I

have no reliance but in Him, and if He falls, I shall fall with Him. But if He does not, I shall not. Because He lives, I shall live also, and I spring to my legs again and fight with my depressions of spirit and get the victory through it. And so may you do, and so you must, for there is no other way of escaping from it."**

Yes, there is no other way. As you contemplate Window 12, let the Holy Spirit arouse in you the blessed assurance that Jesus, your Lord and Savior, is alive and living in you. Blessed be the name of the Lord!

Lord, I often hear people refer to "living in resurrection power!" I'm not sure what all that means, but I do know this: Jesus, you live! You live in my heart. Moment by moment we are working things out for my good. Thank you for being my Savior and risen Lord! Amen.

*Elesha Coffman: Christianity Today, August 2008, "Do You Know the History of the Christian Flag?"

**Charles Haddon Spurgeon (1988). "Spurgeon at His Best: Over 2200 Striking Quotations from the World's Most Exhaustive and Widely-read Sermon Series", Baker Publishing Group

Window 13

Window 13 is somewhat of a mystery. It is intended to portray the ascension of Jesus after his resurrection. Let's read the text of his ascension and then we will discuss the issue this window presents.

Acts 1:1-11:

> [1] In the first book, O Theophilus, I have dealt with all that Jesus began to do and teach, [2] until the day when he was taken up, after he had given commands through the Holy Spirit to the apostles whom he had chosen. [3] He presented himself alive to them after his suffering by many proofs, appearing to them during forty days and speaking about the kingdom of God.
>
> [4] And while staying with them he ordered them not to depart from

Jerusalem, but to wait for the promise of the Father, which, he said, "you heard from me; 5 for John baptized with water, but you will be baptized with the Holy Spirit not many days from now."

6 So when they had come together, they asked him, "Lord, will you at this time restore the kingdom to Israel?" 7 He said to them, "It is not for you to know times or seasons that the Father has fixed by his own authority. 8 But you will receive power when the Holy Spirit has come upon you, and you will be my witnesses in Jerusalem and in all Judea and Samaria, and to the end of the earth." 9 And when he had said these things, as they were looking on, he was lifted up, and a cloud took him out of their sight. 10 And while they were gazing into heaven as he went, behold, two men stood by them in white robes, 11 and said, "Men of Galilee, why do you stand looking into heaven? This Jesus, who was taken up from you into heaven, will come in the same way as you saw him go into heaven."

This is the only Bible reference that refers to the way Jesus ascended into heaven after the resurrection. He remained with his disciples for forty days after the resurrection teaching them things about the kingdom of God, many of which no doubt became teachings in the Epistles.

After he had finished visiting with them on the fortieth day, he rose from the earth and disappeared in a cloud. That is how Jesus ascended into heaven, not in a chariot of fire. So why the chariot of fire? To answer that question let's go way back into the Old Testament and read about Elijah and Elisha. Elijah is about to turn his prophetic ministry over to Elisha, and he does so in a dramatic way.

> *9 When they had crossed, Elijah said to Elisha, "Ask what I shall do for you, before I am taken from you." And Elisha said, "Please let there be a double portion of your spirit on me." 10 And he said, "You have asked a hard thing; yet, if you see me as I am being taken from you, it shall be so for you, but if you do not see me, it shall not be so." 11 And as they still went on and talked, behold, chariots of fire and horses of fire separated the two of them. And Elijah went up by a whirlwind into heaven. 12 And Elisha saw it and he cried, "My father, my father! The chariots of Israel and its horsemen!" And he saw him no more. (2 Kings 2:9-12)*

We see from this passage that it is Elijah who is associated with a chariot of fire as he is taken to heaven. Jesus rose from the earth and disappeared into the clouds.

So why the discrepancy with this window? I can see two possible reasons. First, those who designed the window were not well-versed in the Scriptures and truly thought that Jesus went to heaven in a chariot of fire.

The second possibility I see is that the company that provided the windows did not have a window that specifically illustrated the ascension of Jesus, so they substituted what they thought would be a representation with the chariot of fire. Be that as it may, this window represents the ascension of Jesus to heaven.

The ascension of Jesus to heaven was very important for the church. Jesus had to go to heaven so that the Holy Spirit could be given, which is illustrated in Window 14. As you think about the ascension of Jesus to heaven, pay special attention to the wonderful message that was given to the disciples by the angels following his ascension.

> "Men of Galilee, why do you stand looking into heaven? This Jesus, who

was taken up from you into heaven, will come in the same way as you saw him go into heaven." (Acts 1:11)

From this, we know how Jesus will return, *"in the same way you saw him go."*

When I was a little boy riding in the car one day we saw a light in the sky that was in the shape of a cross and it appeared to be descending. My father said, "Look! Do you think that is Jesus coming back?" It would have been great if it was, but in this case, it was just light reflecting off an airplane. But one day, beloved, Jesus will return in the same way that he left coming down from the sky through the clouds just as he promised. Are you ready? Have you accepted Christ as your Savior? Oh, don't delay. He could come at any time. And it will be a time of great rejoicing for those who have repented of their sins and received Christ as their Savior, but it will be a time of great sorrow for those who have turned away from his love.

Heavenly Father, what a wonderful message the angels gave to the disciples when Jesus rose out of their sight. He's coming back in like manner, and I'm ready! Hallelujah! Amen.

Window 14

We now spend some time looking at Window 14 which depicts the day of Pentecost. This window is a transition from the previous windows. Up until this point each window has represented a specific event in the life of Christ. Although this window involves Christ, he is not physically present but comes in the person of the Holy Spirit. One of the wonderful promises Jesus gave to his disciples is recorded in John chapter 14.

> [15] *"If you love me, you will keep my commandments.* [16] *And I will ask the Father, and he will give you another Helper, to be with you forever,* [17] *even the Spirit of truth, whom the world cannot receive, because it neither sees him nor knows him. You know him, for he dwells with you and will be in you.*

18 "I will not leave you as orphans; I will come to you. 19 Yet a little while and the world will see me no more, but you will see me. Because I live, you also will live. 20 In that day you will know that I am in my Father, and you in me, and I in you. 21 Whoever has my commandments and keeps them, he it is who loves me. And he who loves me will be loved by my Father, and I will love him and manifest myself to him." 22 Judas (not Iscariot) said to him, "Lord, how is it that you will manifest yourself to us, and not to the world?" 23 Jesus answered him, "If anyone loves me, he will keep my word, and my Father will love him, and we will come to him and make our home with him. 24 Whoever does not love me does not keep my words. And the word that you hear is not mine but the Father's who sent me. (John 14:15-24)

Just before his ascension when he rose from the ground and disappeared into the clouds, he gave them some specific instructions.

4 And while staying with them he ordered them not to depart from Jerusalem, but to wait for the promise of the Father, which, he said, "you heard from me; 5 for John baptized with water, but you will be baptized with the

Holy Spirit not many days from now."
(Acts 1:4-5)

That baptism in the Holy Spirit is what Window 14 is all about. Pictured here we see a dove descending from heaven distributing flames of fire, or "tongues" of fire as the scripture states.

> *¹ When the day of Pentecost arrived, they were all together in one place. ² And suddenly there came from heaven a sound like a mighty rushing wind, and it filled the entire house where they were sitting. ³ And divided tongues as of fire appeared to them and rested on each one of them. ⁴ And they were all filled with the Holy Spirit and began to speak in other tongues as the Spirit gave them utterance. (Acts 2:1-4)*

On this day we have come to call "the day of Pentecost" about 120 believers (Acts 1:15) were gathered together. They were following the command Jesus had given them to go and wait for the Holy Spirit. When the day finally arrived they first heard a sound like a howling wind. The Bible doesn't say it was a wind, but the *"sound like a mighty rushing wind"* that filled the entire house. On each one of the believers there appeared what is described as "tongues of fire." Following the wind sound and the tongues of fire, they all began to speak in other tongues or languages; languages that were foreign to them. This had an amazing impact on the people who were in Jerusalem for the Feast of Weeks, which occurred fifty days after the wave offering of Passover.

The Feast of Weeks celebrated the end of the grain harvest. Let us not miss the prophetic connection between the feast of weeks and Pentecost.

"Pentecost took place fifty days after the Feast of Firstfruits.... the Feast of Firstfruits speaks of the resurrection of Jesus Christ. Christ is the firstfruits—"... Christ the firstfruits; afterward they that are Christ's at his coming" (1 Cor. 15:23). The Passover speaks of the death of Jesus Christ, we learn from 1 Corinthians 5:7: "... For even Christ, our Passover is sacrificed for us." Since the Passover has been fulfilled in the death of Christ, and the Feast of Firstfruits has been fulfilled in the resurrection of Christ, we believe that the Feast of Pentecost represents something—that is, it is the fulfillment of something. Its fulfillment is the birth of the

church, the day the church came into existence."*

And what a beginning the church had.

> *⁵ Now there were dwelling in Jerusalem Jews, devout men from every nation under heaven. ⁶ And at this sound, the multitude came together, and they were bewildered because each one was hearing them speak in his own language. ⁷ And they were amazed and astonished, saying, "Are not all these who are speaking Galileans? ⁸ And how is it that we hear, each of us in his own native language? ⁹ Parthians and Medes and Elamites and residents of Mesopotamia, Judea and Cappadocia, Pontus and Asia, ¹⁰ Phrygia and Pamphylia, Egypt and the parts of Libya belonging to Cyrene, and visitors from Rome, ¹¹ both Jews and proselytes, Cretans and Arabians—we hear them telling in our own tongues the mighty works of God." ¹² And all were amazed and perplexed, saying to one another, "What does this mean?" (Acts 2:5-12)*

At this point, Peter addresses the crowd with what we might call the first evangelical, Billy Graham, type sermon. The result was that 3,000 souls were added to the kingdom that day (Acts 2:41).

The question as we look upon this window is, "Have you welcomed the Holy Spirit into your life?" We need power to live and spread the Gospel. The power is not in us, nor is it in the church. It is in the Holy Spirit. So often we fail because we do not recognize this. We need to stop trying to do the work in our own power, but trust him, truly trust him to work all things for our good.

Heavenly Father, I thank you for your Holy Spirit. I want you to know that whatever circumstances I face in life, my faith and trust is in your power to see me through. Amen.

*McGee, J. Vernon. Thru the Bible Commentary, Volumes 1-5: Genesis through Revelation (Thru the Bible 5 Volume Set) (Kindle Locations 105163-105166). Thomas Nelson. Kindle Edition.

Window 15

Do you remember when we observed Window 5, the baptism of Jesus by John the Baptist, we noted the seven beams of light being emitted from the dove? We noted that 7 denotes completeness or perfection in the Bible. Jesus was the complete, sinless man who was to become the "lamb without blemish" as a sacrifice for the sins of all people. Here again, in Window 15 we see that concept displayed in a beautiful way showing Jesus as the Alpha and Omega. Let's explore what that means.

Alpha and Omega is a term that Jesus applied to himself.

> *"I am the Alpha and the Omega," says the Lord God, "who is and who was and*

who is to come, the Almighty."
(Revelation 1:8)

And he said to me, "It is done! I am the Alpha and the Omega, the beginning and the end. To the thirsty, I will give from the spring of the water of life without payment." (Revelation 21:6)

"Behold, I am coming soon, bringing my recompense with me, to repay each one for what he has done. I am the Alpha and the Omega, the first and the last, the beginning and the end." (Revelation 22:12-13)

These words would have been easily interpreted by the Jewish mind. Rabbis taught that something that was complete or whole was Alpha and Omega. Alpha is the first letter of the Greek alphabet and Omega is the last letter.

One of the meanings of Jesus being the "Alpha and Omega" is that He was at the beginning of all things and will be at the close. It is equivalent to saying He always existed and always will exist. It was Christ, as second Person of the Trinity, who brought about the creation: "Through him all things were made; without him nothing was made that has been made" (John 1:3), and His Second Coming will be the beginning of the end of creation as we know it (2 Peter 3:10). As God incarnate, He has no beginning, nor will He have any end with respect to time, being from everlasting to everlasting.

A second meaning of Jesus as the "Alpha and Omega" is that the phrase identifies Him as the God of the Old Testament. Isaiah ascribes this aspect of Jesus' nature as part of the triune God in several places. "I, the Lord, am the first, and with the last I am He" (41:4). "I am the first, and I am the last; and beside me there is no God" (Isaiah 44:6). "I am he; I am the first, I also am the last" (Isaiah 48:12). These are clear indications of the eternal nature of the Godhead.

Christ, as the Alpha and Omega, is the first and last in so many ways. He is the "author and finisher" of our faith (Hebrews 12:2), signifying that He begins it and carries it through to completion. He is the totality, the sum and substance of the Scriptures, both of the Law and of the Gospel (John 1:1, 14). He is the fulfilling end of the Law (Matthew 5:17), and He is the beginning subject matter of the gospel of grace through faith, not of works (Ephesians 2:8-9). He is found in the first *verse of Genesis and in the last verse of Revelation. He is the first and last, the all in all of salvation, from the justification before God to the final sanctification of His people.* *

As we admire this window we also see a scepter, an ornamental staff carried by a king as a symbol of sovereignty. Surrounding the scepter is a crown. These, of course, are references to the fact that Jesus is the King of Kings and Lord of lords. These two items wedged between the Alpha and Omega indicate that Jesus is the final word of all things. No king, dictator, president, or any other ruler can even come close to the sovereignty of our Lord Jesus Christ. Think about that! Jesus Christ, our Savior, Lord, and coming King is so much more than all the power and glory you can muster any place in the world past, present or future.

Not only that but as we shall see in the final window, we too, are kings and priests of God having been adopted into his family by the sacrifice of Jesus upon the cross. Do you feel special yet? I hope so.

Lord, in a world where the struggle for power is so prevalent, it is good to know that in Christ I have everything. Thank

you for being my Alpha and Omega. Amen.

* Alpha and Omega, gotquestions.org.

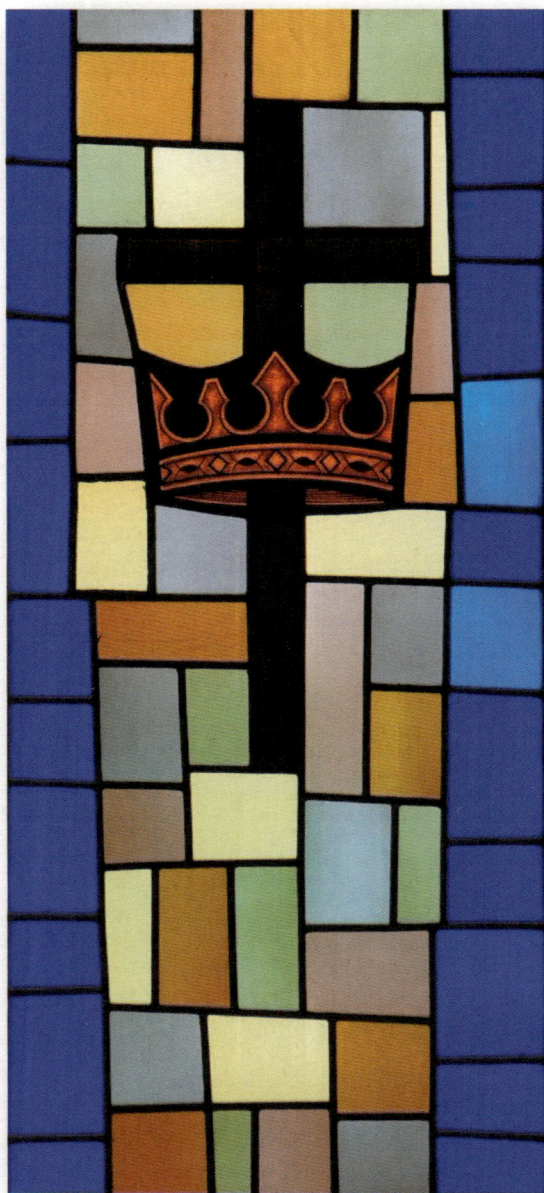

Window 16

In this our final stained-glass window in the series, we have depicted before us a cross and crown. The Cross and Crown is a familiar symbol in Christian churches. It represents the reward awaiting in heaven (the crown) that believers will receive after the suffering and trials of life on earth (the cross).

> *Blessed is the man who remains steadfast under trial, for when he has stood the test, he will receive the crown of life, which God has promised to those who love him. (James 1:12)*

Remaining steadfast under trial implies that we will suffer in this life. Anyone who has lived for any length of time knows that life is not easy. Sometimes it's the pits! Embracing the idea that suffering is part and parcel of life goes a long way to helping us to endure.

Read these words of Jesus:

> *"I have said these things to you, that in me you may have peace. In the world, you will have tribulation. But take heart; I have overcome the world." (John 16:33)*

The presence of suffering in our life is a vivid reminder that we have not yet reached our heavenly home; a home described in Revelation 21.

> *"Behold, the dwelling place of God is with man. He will dwell with them, and they will be his people, and God himself will be with them as their God. He will wipe away every tear from their eyes, and death shall be no more, neither shall there be mourning, nor crying, nor pain anymore, for the former things have passed away." (Revelation 21:3-4)*

What a glorious day that will be! And that's what this window represents.

In the meantime, let us understand that our suffering here is not just random or without purpose. God has a plan for your life.

> *For I know the plans I have for you, declares the Lord, plans for welfare and not for evil, to give you a future and a hope. Then you will call upon me and*

*come and pray to me, and I will hear
you. You will seek me and find me when
you seek me with all your heart.
(Jeremiah 29:11-13)*

While you are waiting for the crown of life, you need to understand that even in the midst your suffering God is at work. You also need to understand that your suffering is not intended to be alone. You have a fellowship of believing brothers and sisters to lean upon and to share in suffering.

"Christians still suffer as we wait for Jesus to return, but none of our suffering is random or without purpose.

The church is not meant to be a loosely bound association of functional Lone Rangers. Paul confronts that type of thinking when he writes, "Bear one another's burdens, and so fulfill the law of Christ" (Galatians 6:2).

The church is meant to be a refuge for those suffering. When a member is hurting, the church applies the bandages; when a member is down, the church encourages; when a member is in need, the church comes alongside to help."*

This is one of the reasons why these windows are so important in our church. Yes, our church is made of steel, brick-and-mortar, wood, and a lot of other materials including the glass that is used in the windows, and we acknowledge that the actual "church" is the people who attend. But God has gifted people to construct beautiful buildings that aesthetically draw our attention to God. And these windows serve to do that in a powerful way. When we come to worship, they serve as a constant reminder of Christ and what he has done for us. They lead us all the way from his birth through the cross and the resurrection to the crown of life that we will receive when this life is over, and we enter our heavenly home.

In the meantime, this window illustrates the special status we have in the Kingdom of God. In Revelation 5 while worshipping around the throne of God, the twenty-four elders sang about it.

> *9 And they sang a new song, saying,*
> *"Worthy are you to take the scroll*
>   *and to open its seals,*
> *for you were slain, and by your blood*
> *you ransomed people for God*
>   *from every tribe and language and*
> *people and nation,*
> *10 and you have made them a kingdom*
> *and priests to our God,*

and they shall reign on the earth."
(Revelation 5:9-10)

Do you see yourself in that song? I hope so. If you are a believer in the Lord Jesus you are part of the *"ransomed people,"* and that places you in the group of *"priests to our God."* In other words, we are to live in victory, overcoming the powers of darkness and despair. We are the light of the world, the salt of the earth. Let's live for Jesus and share his love with all we meet.

My Father in heaven, thank you that I am part of the "ransomed people" spoken of in the book of Revelation. I pray that I will be faithful to share the love of Jesus with others, letting my light shine with Jesus as we overcome the powers of darkness. Amen.

*Joseph Scheumann: desiringgod.org, "Five Truths About Christian Suffering

Go Forth to Serve

Rear Window

There is one more window to add to our sanctuary windows. Although this window is not part of the original life of Christ series, it has become a very meaningful window due to its location and message.

Designed by the author of this book and constructed by Classic Art Glass Company of Omaha, Nebraska, this window was installed in 2005 and serves as a challenge to each congregant as they exit the sanctuary.

The dove symbolizes the Holy Spirit, and the hands, the hands of God, reminding each one that we are to be his loving hands, in the power of the Holy Spirit, to the world around us. A wooden plaque below the window is engraved with the words, "Go Forth to Serve."

Made in the USA
Columbia, SC
15 July 2018